Socially DISTANT,
Spiritually CLOSE

Socially Distant, Spiritually Close

A Perpetual Advent Devotional

SHERYL VASSO *and* SUSAN WEBER

XULON PRESS

Xulon Press
2301 Lucien Way #415
Maitland, FL 32751
407.339.4217
www.xulonpress.com

Unless otherwise indicated, Scripture quotations taken from the English Standard Version (ESV). Copyright © 2001 by Crossway, a publishing ministry of Good News Publishers. Used by permission. All rights reserved.

Paperback ISBN-13: 978-1-6628-3101-0

In gratitude to the Grace Point, Newtown, PA Wednesday morning Bible Study members. Thank you for making Wednesday the best day of the week and keeping us focused on God's worthy Word.

TABLE OF CONTENTS

DEAR FRIENDS,

*A*s we were writing this devotional, the world was in the midst of the pandemic of 2020, which changed many things in our lives, not the least of which was how we celebrated Christmas. Words and phrases such as, "unprecedented" and "social distancing", crept into our language and became very commonplace. The world moved from red to yellow, and in some cases, to green phases of reopening, but the hopeful thought of celebrating Christmas in a totally green phase was unrealized. We celebrated Christmas in a *socially distant* manner.

Many of us could not wait to turn the calendar from 2020 to 2021, thinking that flipping the calendar page would also "flip the switch" to a return to normal, and that somehow we would be out of the pandemic. However, well into 2021 we are still dealing with the pandemic, vaccinations, and now a variant of the virus that could prove to be more deadly than our introduction to Covid-19! Yes, the world is opening up again and many aspects of life feel more normal, but there are still pockets of *social distancing* in effect.

Regardless of how the global pandemic plays out in the years to come, and regardless of how social distancing may fade away, we want to encourage you to remain spiritually close to one another and to our Heavenly Father. Thus our devotional, *Socially Distant, Spiritually Close!*

Many Christian families, churches, and individual followers of Jesus, observe the annual season of Advent, even though no biblical mandate exists to do so. It is a time of preparation for the coming of Christmas Day, as the English word, "Advent", originates from the Latin word, "Adventus", and means "coming". The first coming of Jesus was two millennia ago, and it is that first coming we have in view each Advent season, although Jesus' second coming is in sight as well.

Christians celebrate Advent in different ways: some light candles, some sing songs, some eat cookies, and some give gifts. What an enjoyable and spiritually profitable way to extend celebrating Jesus' coming beyond the short 24 hours of Christmas Day! After all, the birth of Christ, the incarnation of the Son of God, is too great an event to accomplish in only 24 hours.

Please join us as we anticipate and celebrate the coming of Christ this Christmas. The **GIVING**, the **GATHERING**, and the **GAIETY** of celebrating may require some social distancing now and in the years to come. However, **GOD WITH US** has made it possible to remain spiritually close to each other and to our heavenly Father. ***SOCIALLY DISTANT, SPIRITUALLY CLOSE!***

Sheryl and Susan

Week One
"GIVING"

Sheryl Vasso

GIVING

*N*etflix binging most likely replaced baseball as America's favorite pastime during the pandemic of 2020. I certainly did my share of watching Netflix during Covid-19, however, the watching of American Sitcoms from the 60s surpassed my Netflix viewing. One sitcom, in particular, captured my attention –"Father Knows Best"!

In one episode, Jim, the father who typically knew best about any situation, was disappointed in his family's attitude toward Christmas. His oldest daughter was attempting to drop a hint to her boyfriend as to what she wanted for Christmas, while his youngest daughter wanted a pink tree instead of a traditional green tree. Above all, his son was blasting Christmas carols as an advertising scheme to sell used cars because his boss claimed, "Christmas was the best time to sell stuff!"

In frustration, Jim exclaimed, "Why can't we have Christmas the way it used to be? Quiet! Simple! A few friends and family sitting around the fire, kids hanging their stockings over the fireplace, Christmas bells ringing on Christmas Eve, carolers singing! Have you forgotten everything you learned in Sunday school? ALL THIS

FOLDEROL! Why not grab an ax, go out into the country, and chop down our own Christmas tree?"

That is exactly what the family did, amidst the children's protests that they needed to be back in the early evening for various activities. However, the family encountered an unexpected snowstorm which kept them stranded in a cabin in the middle of nowhere without all the frills or FOLDEROL of Christmas. It is in that cabin, and during that Christmas Eve, that the family adjusted their attitudes and remembered what is most meaningful about Christmas.

It is quite easy for all of us get lost in ALL THIS FOLDEROL of **GIVING** presents, of **GATHERING** with family and friends, and of traditions of **GAIETY** that surround Christmas. While much of what Jim Anderson calls "folderol" is perfectly acceptable and exciting, it is good for all of us to remember the true meaning of Christmas, that **GOD IS WITH US,** and how His presence began with **GIVING**!

"For to us a child is born, to us a son is given;"

Isaiah 9:6

"For God so loved the world, that he gave his only Son, that whoever believes in him should not perish but have eternal life."

John 3:16

"No Good Thing"
December 1

*D*o you remember Santa Claus riding through the neighborhoods on a fire truck during the weeks before Christmas? The first hint that he was coming was the din of sirens in the distance, which did not indicate an emergency alarm, but rather, the arrival of Santa Claus.

Santa's coming to town on a firetruck stirred up a mix of emotions within my young heart—a mix of fun and fright. The fun was that Santa was paying a visit; the fright was that "he knows what you've been doing" and "whether you've been bad or good"! It was frightening enough to give even a small child high blood pressure! Regardless, I can remember grabbing a coat and hurrying to get outside so as not to miss the "candy toss" that Santa would perform. In addition, I can remember jockeying for position and getting in line with Santa's pitch so I would not miss catching any of what Santa was throwing.

My childhood memory is refreshed each Christmas season when Santa comes through the neighborhood, in which I now live. I hear the sirens in the distance, and even though it has been years since I was a child, I can still distinguish the fire alarm from the alarm signaling

Santa's arrival. Each year, I still run outside, not to catch my own candy, but to catch a view of my neighbors gathering their children and lining them up closely for the Santa "candy toss". It is still great fun to see Santa come to town!

However, it is no longer frightening when he comes because my mind goes to a different place than when I was a child. My mind ponders **Psalm 84:11**$_b$,

> *"No good thing does He withhold*
> *from those who walk uprightly."*

As God's children walk sincerely and rightly, God will withhold no thing that is valuable, good, and merry, from them. Never do God's children need to jockey for position, or make sure they get in the line of God's giving of good things. If we are walking uprightly, we need not fear that anything good for us will miss us—a job, a promotion, a spouse, etc… What a comfort to know that the God who knows all of what I have been doing, whether bad or good, will never withhold that which is good for me as I walk rightly with Him!

Read: Psalm 84

Reflect: Are you being careful to walk uprightly before the Lord? If so, are you trusting Him to give you everything that is good for you? How does Psalm 84 cause you to trust the Lord to satisfy your longings?

"Batteries Not Included"
December 2

O ne of my favorite places to do my Christmas shopping is *Bed Bath & Beyond*, due to one of their most endearing consumer friendly services. At checkout, they provide notification of how many batteries your purchase requires. Not only do they do the battery alert thing well, they make the purchasing of said batteries very convenient. Visibly hanging next to the cash register, alongside Orbit and Trident gum packs, as well as the latest *People Magazine*, are a variety of battery sizes and quantities for your automatic hand soap dispenser, electric toothbrush or just purchased toy!

After years of buying battery operated toys for my nieces and nephews, especially at Christmas time, I finally caught on to how annoying my gift giving was to my brothers and sisters-in-law because of failing to include the necessary batteries with my gift. My forgetfulness in the power supply area placed a huge burden on my relatives to find batteries IMMEDIATELY lest their children be surrounded by useless, non-functioning toys! I had good intentions in the AA and AAA area and often remembered to buy the batteries, but just as often, forgot to wrap them up with my gifts or bring them along to the family gatherings. I now understand the frustration I caused because I know what it is like to buy something for myself and be "battery-less". The item is useless without the power!

God gets this too! In **2 Peter 1:3** we read, *"His divine power has granted to us all things that pertain to life and godliness…"* He provides everything we need, not some of what we need, or most of what we need, but ALL that we need to live a godly life. He gives us the power and then tells us, in the following verses, to be diligent and make haste to add qualities of moral excellence, knowledge, self-control, perseverance, godliness, brotherly kindness, and love to our faith (**2 Peter 1:5–7**). His divine power empowers us to live a godly life that will make us useful and fruitful for His purposes and glory.

It would be wonderful if vendors, instead of going to the trouble of printing "requires 2 AA batteries not included" on the package, would just include them in the first place! Life would be so much easier if **ALL** the power needed to make our gadgets useful and fully functional, were provided at point of purchase!

> *"For if these qualities are yours and are increasing, they keep you from being ineffective or unfruitful in the knowledge of our Lord Jesus Christ."*

> **2 Peter 1:8**

Read: 2 Peter 1:1–21

Reflect: What areas of your spiritual life feel powerless or run down (knowledge of His word? kindness towards others?). What has God promised He would do to empower you?

"Every Good and Perfect Gift"
December 3

*D*o you struggle every Christmas with finding good and perfect gifts along with the perfect balance of gift giving? Do you struggle with what to give to the person who has everything, or how much to give to express how much someone means to you? How do you give the good and perfect gift without breaking the bank, and without being caught up in materialism and consumerism?

Year after year, I would struggle with this, until finally one year I saw what I thought was the perfect and good gift-giving guide! The article I saw was entitled something like, *Simplify Gift Giving this Year* and the suggestion was to give to your children, in particular, a gift in each of four categories—something they WANT, something to READ, something to WEAR, and something they NEED. I thought it was great and so I followed the advice and it made gift giving so much easier. It helped me to give meaningfully, significantly, and abundantly without going *overboard*, if you know what I mean.

When I was a little kid, my best friend next door had what I would consider an *overboard* Christmas each year. It started with their Christmas tree, which could have been the perfect substitute for the

Trafalgar Square tree given by Norway each year to England. Under the enormous tree were so many piles of gifts that it looked as though their living room was a Macy's store location!

Speaking of Macy's, who of us has not camped out at a department store or two in order to buy the gift of the year for our kids? I remember when Cabbage patch dolls were all the rage—the demand for them was high but the birth rate was low. So parents stood in lines waiting for the doors of the store to open and all the fruit of the Spirit went by the wayside as the dark underbelly of our personalities took over. We yanked gifts out of people's hands and stomped all over other human beings –whatever it took to get the gift!

The Bible compares our giving of gifts to our children to how God gives gifts to His children.

> *"⁹Or which one of you, if his son asks him for bread, will give him a stone? ¹⁰Or if he asks for a fish, will give him a serpent? ¹¹If you then, who are evil, know how to give good gifts to your children, how much more will your Father who is in heaven give good things to those who ask him!"*

> **Matthew 7:9–11**

Even in our human frailty and finiteness, we know how to give appropriately—bread instead of stones. We know how ***not*** to give inappropriately—we do not give a serpent—something harmful—in place of fish—something helpful to our children. However, **HOW MUCH MORE** will your Father who is in heaven give good things to those who ask Him! God, who does not need a gift-giving guide from Pinterest, knows how to give bread and good and perfect gifts to us.

Read: James 1:17

Reflect: From whom do we receive every good and perfect gift? What characteristic of God makes His gifts so amazing and valuable?

"Regifting or Degifting?"
December 4

egifting is the act of taking a received gift and giving it to somebody else, often in the guise of a new gift. It has become such a practice that the USA has declared December 18 as "National Regifting Day", and Canada has marketed December 26–30, as "National Regifting Week". Today, there are even websites and apps available to assist you in turning your unwanted gifts into cash. In case you are interested in a side job this year, candles, picture frames, and yes, fruitcake, make the top 10 list of the most *regifted* presents.

I am not a Seinfeld Sitcom buff by any means, but I recently caught an episode from Season 6, entitled, "The Label Maker", which apparently popularized the term, *"regifting"*. Jerry had Super Bowl tickets, which he could not use because he was in a wedding on Super Bowl Sunday. Therefore, he gave his tickets to his dentist friend, Dr. Tim Whatley, who in turn thanked Jerry by giving him a label maker. One day, Elaine, Jerry's friend, visits Jerry in his apartment, sees the label maker, and exclaims what a great gadget it is and how she had given one recently to Dr. Tim in exchange for free dental work he had performed on her impacted molar. Learning that Dr. Tim is the one who sent Jerry the gift, and why, Elaine connects the dots and declares that Dr. Tim is a *"regifter"*! As the story continues, the wedding on Super Bowl Sunday gets canceled, which frees Jerry to go to the game for which he no longer has tickets. Therefore, Jerry's friends encourage Jerry to call Dr. Tim and ask for the tickets back because "if he can *regift*, you can *degift!*"

Whether you are a *regifter* or not, one thought that brings great comfort is that God is neither a *regifter* nor *degifter*. In **Romans 11:29**, Paul states this principle,

"For the gifts and the calling of God are irrevocable."

While the context of this verse is particularly relevant to the nation and ethnicity of Israel, the application is still true for those of us who have accepted the greatest gift ever given—the gift of eternal life through Jesus Christ the son of God!

"For the wages of sin is death, but the free gift of God is eternal life in Christ Jesus our Lord."

Romans 6:23

"20 For all the promises of God find their Yes in him (Jesus Christ). That is why it is through him that we utter our Amen to God for his glory. 21 And it is God who establishes us with you in Christ, and has anointed us, 22 and who has also put his seal on us and given us his Spirit in our hearts as a guarantee."

2 Corinthians 1:20–22

Take comfort this holiday season—once you receive the gift of eternal life through Jesus Christ, God will never *"de-gift"* you!

Read: Ephesians 1:13–14; Romans 8:39

Reflect: Who seals our salvation? For how long? What can separate us from the love of God?

"But where are the Nine?"
December 5

"In everything give thanks: for this is the will of God in Christ Jesus concerning you."

I Thessalonians 5:18 (NASB)

"For everything write thank you notes: for this is the will of your Mother concerning you."

The Book of Gloria Vasso

My mother is a devout believer in writing "thank you" notes. Every birthday and Christmas, my mother would prompt my writing of "thank you" notes for all the gifts given to me on those occasions. It was something she has instilled in me since I was very young and I am most grateful, because giving thanks is the will of "God in Christ Jesus concerning you".

In **Luke 17:11–17** we read of ten lepers who lifted up their voices and said,

"¹¹On the way to Jerusalem he was passing along between Samaria and Galilee. ¹²And as he entered a village, he was met by ten lepers, who stood at a distance ¹³and lifted up their voices, saying, 'Jesus, Master, have mercy on us.' ¹⁴When he saw them he said to them, 'Go and show yourselves to the priests.' And as they went they were cleansed. ¹⁵Then one of them, when he saw that he was healed, turned back, praising God with a loud voice; ¹⁶and he fell on his face at Jesus' feet, giving him thanks. Now he was a Samaritan. ¹⁷Then Jesus answered, 'Were not ten cleansed? Where are the nine?'"

In addition to mothers around the world, God desires for His children to possess an attitude of gratitude, as it is a key ingredient for joyful living. However, if gratitude is so vital why is it that not everyone is grateful? Perhaps, it is because many obstacles exist to being grateful, and chief among them may be a sense of entitlement, which suggests that others owe us, or that we deserve something from somebody else. With this mentality, even if we receive something, it is not a *gift* but a *right*.

Another obstacle to gratitude is familiarity. The more we have exposure to a particular blessing in life, the more likely we are to take it for granted. Again, as a result, we begin to feel entitled and less grateful. Even though we may delight in the Word of God daily, we need to guard against feeling overexposed to it, or taking it for granted.

I hope that this Christmas season of giving, we will purpose in our hearts to express our thankfulness. Never do we want to be like the nine who failed to glorify God by returning thanks to Him for His unending mercies.

Read: Psalm 103

Reflect: What blessings from God cause you the most gratitude? How do you express your gratefulness to God? How can you have a more expressive attitude of gratitude towards God and others? Are there some "thank yous" you need to write or say in person?

"The Great Exchange"
December 6

xchanging Christmas gifts, we have received from others, is almost inevitable. Even though great thought may have gone into choosing the perfect gift for someone, our gift may not completely satisfy the recipient. The gift may not be the proper fit, color, brand, or model. Perhaps the recipient of our gift is not a "regifter" or "degifter", but, rather, an "exchanger". Nowadays, retail stores, even those online, make exchanging very convenient and private. Thanks to gift receipts, the giver of the gift does not even have to know their gift was exchanged. Could it be any easier?

Even though exchanging gifts during the Christmas season is almost inevitable, there is a "Great Exchange" that may go unnoticed. It is the exchange that Jesus Christ made for the world! In **John 3:16** we read of God's extraordinary love for the world.

> *"For God so loved the world, that he gave his only Son, that whoever believes in him should not perish but have eternal life."*

Jesus Christ exchanged His life for our sins so that we all may have eternal life! All of us have said things, done things, or thought things that are wrong, and in so doing we have sinned (**Romans 3:23** – *"… for all have sinned and fall short of the glory of God,"*). Scripture tells us there is a penalty to be paid for our sins, and that penalty is death.

> *"For the wages of sin is death, but the free gift of God is eternal life in Christ Jesus our Lord."*

Romans 6:23

Notice the free gift of eternal life mentioned in that verse. Jesus Christ shed His blood on the cross for our sins, paid our penalty in full, so that we could have eternal life. What a great exchange! Jesus' blood for our sins! Eternal life in exchange for death!

Whether you have ever made a Christmas gift exchange or not, please do not miss the Greatest Exchange—God's free gift of eternal life through the shed blood of His only Son, Christ Jesus our Lord!

If you have already made this exchange, why not pass on the good news to someone who has not? It will be the greatest Christmas gift ever given and received! It cannot be **degifted** once received, and there will never be a desire to exchange this free gift once accepted. It is truly a gift that will keep on giving for all eternity!

Read: 1 John 5:13–15

Reflect: How do these verses encourage us to abide by what we *KNOW* rather than by what we *FEEL?* What is it that we can *KNOW* for sure?

Week Two
"GATHERING"

Susan Weber

GATHERING

This Advent week we are focusing on gathering. Christmas is a time for gathering. We gather at church for Advent services, Cantatas, Christmas Eve, and other special events. We gather in our homes with family and friends. We gather in our communities for tree lightings and concerts. Our society places great emphasis on holiday happenings. We love to celebrate the holidays with others.

The year 2020 brought a new perspective to gatherings. Once ignored coughs and sneezes, now bring thoughts of wide spread disease. We have developed heightened concerns about being in large groups. Quarantines and masks are now part of our norm and we expect restrictions to be placed on events like those placed in London during the pandemic. It was illegal to visit in another person's home, or even to dine with people with whom you did not reside. Although many of these regulations have since been lifted, their existence serves as a reminder to be careful in gathering.

Just as the pandemic made us focus on *how* we gathered, we also need to be careful about *why* we gather. Oftentimes our Christmas events are not focused on Christ. They are social events highlighting the secular aspects of the holiday rather than the spiritual ones. The pandemic gave us the opportunity to be intentional about the events we attended. The worries and concerns of that experience made us more conscious of safety, and we became more particular about where, when, and how we gathered. We also need to be intentional about why we gather at Christmas, and make Christ the focus of each event.

Christmas gatherings may also be sorrowful for some. Depression and loneliness, can at times, arrive with the holiday. Memories or expectations highlight the loss of a loved one or unfulfilled hopes. Christmas 2020 was a lonely experience for many as they missed the companionship of others, or a special loved one. It is good to remember that our joy in the holiday season does not rest in gatherings at church, or with family and friends. While those gatherings can bring us happiness, our real joy is not found in others or places. The good news, that Christ has come to save the world, is the true joy of Christmas. Our joy should not be diminished by the circumstances of each Christmas season. Paul's words in **1 Thessalonians 5:16–18** are a good reminder.

> "*16Rejoice always, 17pray without ceasing, 18give thanks in all circumstances; for this is the will of God in Christ Jesus for you.*"

Rejoice always. Rejoice this Christmas despite the circumstances. Rejoice in the gatherings you can attend. Rejoice because yearly Christmas celebrations change, but the good news of Christmas is the same yesterday, today, and forever!

"What are you waiting for?"
December 7

ecember 7th is the day President Franklin Roosevelt declared would live in infamy. On that day in 1941, Japan attacked the United States at Pearl Harbor. It was also my mother's 21st birthday. She heard the news while drying the Sunday dinner dishes at her grandmother's house. It was distressing news for the nation, and for herself, as she had a young beau who could be called off to war. I am sure she spent the next four years waiting for the war to be over, and anticipating life in peace once again.

December is a month for waiting and anticipating. Young children are waiting for Santa, and older children are anticipating their gifts. Young adults are anticipating parties and events. Moms and Grandmas are anticipating perfect family gatherings. Each one is anticipating a perfect Christmas event. They spend endless hours preparing, often with high expectations, for the best Christmas ever.

My big family event is on Christmas Eve day. On December 24th, my husband and I gather with our two sons and their families. I spend weeks planning the menu, decorating, and purchasing gifts. I start early, gathering gifts, and that usually results in too many, although my grandchildren would argue that wasn't true. I begin decorating immediately after Thanksgiving, and my favorite part is hanging twelve stockings on the mantel. The stockings are a daily reminder of the joy we will find in celebrating Christmas and being together. Anticipating and waiting are part of the celebration of Christmas.

The Bible speaks of two people who were waiting and anticipating the birth of the Messiah. Simeon was a devout, righteous man, who was waiting to see the fulfillment of God's promise.

The Holy Spirit had revealed to him that he would witness this event before his death. The prophetess Anna, was also waiting for the Messiah. She and Simeon were at the temple the day Mary and Joseph came to dedicate their newborn baby son. They recognized the child as the Christ. **Luke 2:38** tells us,

> *"And coming up at that very hour she began to give thanks to God and to speak of Him to all who were waiting for the redemption of Jerusalem."*

Both Simeon and Anna recognized the Christ and gave thanks. Their waiting was over.

What are you anticipating this Christmas? What are you waiting for? Some of us are anticipating all the festivities of a traditional holiday. Others are waiting for a "new normal" celebration and are apprehensive about what that will be. Still others are feeling lonely and depressed, as capturing past Christmases is no longer possible. Some feel they have nothing to anticipate, and some are anticipating the wrong thing.

May we learn from Anna and Simeon to focus on God's promises. The anticipation of Christmas is a reminder that the Lord is come and He is coming again. Do not focus on the wrong thing this year. Anticipate Christ this Christmas and not the holiday. Do not sacrifice the anticipation of Christ for the anticipation of an event.

Isaiah 26:8

"In the path of Your judgments, O LORD, we wait for You; Your name and remembrance are the desire of our soul."

Read: Luke 2:22–38

* ✳ Just as Anna and Simeon were awaiting the coming of the Messiah, how might we await the approach of this Christmas with a focus on Christ?
* ✳ How might we await the second coming of Christ?

Reflect: Think about your family gatherings this year. How does that gathering help you anticipate and celebrate the birth of Christ? How can you be intentional about focusing on Him at this event? Many substitute the traditional holiday dessert for a birthday cake for Jesus. Others swap the Hollywood seasonal movie for one of Christ's birth. Perhaps you need to substitute reading *The Night before Christmas* for a reading of the historical event in God's Word. Make Christ the center of your Christmas gatherings.

"Spending Time with a Friend"
December 8

*F*riends are another essential element of Christmas gatherings, but sometimes it is not possible to gather with them. That was the case in 2020 when the Covid pandemic isolated us from others. I remember receiving a group text from a friend that December. It was a picture of the Mona Lisa with a facemask on and the tag line was, "I miss your smiling faces". We do miss our friends when the situation keeps us apart, especially during the Christmas season.

The 2020 Covid pandemic changed how we could celebrate and meet with friends. Gatherings were limited to smaller numbers and we were asked to meet outside rather than inside. Yielding to caution, we refrained from embracing others as we once freely did. Although we missed our friends, we guarded our personal bubbles. We feared what they might bring into our "world".

Although we may miss our earthly friends when circumstances arise, we often overlook another friend at Christmas – a heavenly one! This is odd because it is His birthday. In **John 15**, Jesus calls us His friends. In verses **13–15** Jesus says,

"¹³Greater love has no one than this, that someone lay down his life for his friends. ¹⁴You are my friends if you do what I command you. ¹⁵No longer do I call you servants, for the servant does not know what his master is doing; but I have called you friends, for all that I have heard from My Father I have made known to you."

Christmas is the birthday of our friend, Jesus. He demonstrated His friendship by giving His life for us. In return, we show our friendship by obeying His commandments. I love how He calls us friends and not servants. We refer to serving Him, but He regards that service as something we do for a friend. Jesus calls us friends and makes known to us all that God has revealed to Him. Christ holds nothing back from us.

So how can we celebrate our Friend on His birthday this year? The last verse in Christina Rossetti's poem, *In the Bleak Midwinter*, reads,

> What can I give Him,
> Poor as I am?
> If I were a shepherd
> I would bring a lamb,
> If I were a Wise Man
> I would do my part,—
> Yet what I can I give Him,
> Give my heart.

Perhaps you have done that. You have given Christ your heart. If you have not, there is no better time than Christmas to do so. If you have, why not determine to spend more time with Christ? We love spending time with friends. Jesus loves spending time with you. Open up His Word and get to know Him better. Is there any better way to celebrate a friend's birthday than spending time in their presence, or giving them the gift they most want to receive? Jesus is waiting to be your friend.

SOCIALLY DISTANT, SPIRITUALLY CLOSE | 29

Psalm 25:14

"The friendship of the Lord is for those who fear him, and he makes known to them his covenant."

Read: John 15:13–15

* ❊ How has Jesus been a friend to you?
* ❊ How might you demonstrate your friendship with Christ?

Reflect: This Christmas focus on celebrating your friend Jesus' birth. What can you do to honor Him this year? Some friends post messages on Facebook, give to a charity in their friend's name, or simply create a special time to share together. How can you honor Christ on His birthday?

"Observe CHRISTmas"
December 9

During the Covid-19 pandemic quarantine, my husband and I started watching old television shows. Since we have close friends in Scranton, PA, we were drawn to *The Office*, which is set in Scranton. We had never watched this show before, although we had been to the "museum" at Cooper's Seafood House in that city. The "*Office*" employees are constantly having parties. There was not an event they did not celebrate, and, of course, each of the nine seasons had a Christmas party. Just like on the TV show, holiday parties have become part of our Christmas traditions. These parties are quite interesting because, although intended to be Christmas parties, not all of the workers are Christians. Nevertheless, celebrating Christmas in the office has become a holiday event.

Each year many of us attend Christmas celebrations of this nature. Whether held at the office, in schools, or any public place, people come together for fellowship and enjoyment of the season. These gatherings give us a great opportunity to share the good news of Christmas with others.

Or do they? How often do we use this opportunity to spread the good news of Christ's birth? Perhaps, like for me, it was just another task on the holiday "to do" list. I know I was so wrapped up in Christmas preparations that office cookie exchanges, purchasing gifts for colleagues, and preparing my contribution to the Christmas party, were merely tasks totally unassociated with celebrating Christ's birth. I saved the real focus of Christmas for later at the Christmas Eve service.

It seems that many of us spend a whole month celebrating Christmas, but only one day celebrating Christ's birth. We get wrapped up in holiday associated tasks and events and do not stop and focus on Christ. However, we were given an assignment as workers in God's kingdom. **Matthew 28:16–20** says,

> "16 Now the eleven disciples went to Galilee, to the mountain to which Jesus had directed them. 17 And when they saw Him they worshiped Him, but some doubted. 18 And Jesus came and said to them, 'All authority in heaven and on earth has been given to Me. 19 Go therefore and make disciples of all nations, baptizing them in the name of the Father and of the Son and of the Holy Spirit, 20 teaching them to observe all that I have commanded you. And behold, I am with you always, to the end of the age.'"

We have the task of teaching others to observe all that Christ commanded, and that would include teaching who Christ is. The miracles surrounding his birth are a testimony to who Christ is and this is an opportunity to remind others of what we believe.

So this year think intentionally of how you can include Christ in the contacts you have with your colleagues. In the past, were you careful to send "holiday" cards so as not to offend others?

Perhaps this year your greeting should include Biblical references and not human traditions. Maybe you could invite colleagues to attend a church service or spiritual event with you. Think of ways God is opening doors for you to share Christ this Christmas.

When I was a Sunday school student, we sang a chorus called, *Sermon in Shoes*. We sang about walking and talking, living and giving, teaching and preaching, and knowing and showing the Gospel to all those around us. In those days, we used flannel graph, and those verbs were all on shoes and everyone in the class would spiritedly volunteer to put our shoe word into action during the song. This Christmas, put your shoes into action and "walk/talk", "live/give", "teach/preach", and "know/show" the Good News of Christ to others.

I Corinthians 3:9

"For we are God's fellow workers. You are God's field, God's building."

Read: Matthew 28:16–20

* What task did Christ give to his followers?
* How are you doing with this task?

Reflect: Be intentional this year to let others know you are celebrating Christ's birth. This is not a holiday about the world's love, but God's Love. This is not a holiday about gifts, but God's Gift. This is not a holiday about good times, but Good News. Be intentional to share that with others.

"Vain Celebrations"
December 10

$\mathcal{E}$ach December I look forward to attending the Washington Crossing Chapter of *The Daughters of the American Revolution* Christmas luncheon. It is usually a very elegant affair held in a charming restaurant bedecked for the holiday season. This function also features a charity component. The members bring a batch of their favorite festive cookies to exchange. Only in this case, we purchase the cookies and the funds support community projects. It is quite a lovely event which our members await with pleasure.

Many organizations feature a holiday event during this month. From local spin classes to national organizations, every group cele-brates the holiday season. However, many are celebrating the "spirit" of the holiday while managing to remove Christ from the event. So I ask the question, "Is it really Christmas without Christ?"

I was recently studying Tony Evans' work on the power of God's name. He refers to **Exodus 20:7** which says,

"You shall not take the name of the Lord your God in vain, for the Lord will not hold him guiltless who takes His name in vain."

I wonder if each time we celebrate Christmas without focusing on Christ, we are taking His name in vain.

In **Matthew 1:21**, an angel appears to Joseph and says that Mary *"… will bear a son, and you shall call his name Jesus, for he will save his people from their sins."* The name of Jesus means Savior. He is the Christ, the Messiah, the one who came from God to save us from our sins. Each time we celebrate Christmas without focusing on Christ, we are overlooking the wonderful sacrifice of our Lord. There is no Christmas without Christ, and to celebrate otherwise is to celebrate in vain.

The world focuses on a "spirit" of love at this season. Our society chooses to focus on ways man can show love and often forgets the great love of God. **John 3:16** reminds us *"For God so loved the world, that he gave his only Son, that whoever believes in him should not perish but have eternal life."* The gift of Jesus needs to be the focus of our celebrations this year and every year. The name of Jesus should be spoken often and praised frequently during our gatherings. May we exalt His name as God intended.

In **Philippians 2:9–11** Paul wrote,

> *"9 Therefore God has highly exalted him and bestowed on him the name that is above every name, 10 so that at the name of Jesus every knee should bow, in heaven and on earth and under the earth, 11 and every tongue confess that Jesus Christ is Lord, to the glory of God the Father."*

May we also exalt the name of Jesus this Christmas. May our celebration be one that demonstrates our joy in the birth of our Lord, our

King and our Savior. May all that we do this Christmas season bring honor to His name.

Read: Isaiah 9:6

✷ What does the name Jesus mean to you?
✷ How can you promote His name this Christmas season?

Reflect: Keep Christ in Christmas. May it be apparent you are celebrating His birth. Avoid the short cut of *Xmas* and the use of secular images to denote the holiday. Bring Christ to every holiday event. Celebrate His sacrificial spirit and the love He showed in giving His life for us.

"Sing His Praise"
December 11

ℰℯℴℯℴℯ

Each year our church holds the Women's Christmas Tea. Since I am a tea drinker, I love this affair. Tea drinkers are often overlooked in our Starbucks and Dunkin' world, but the Christmas tea is a tea drinker's paradise. It is a lovely event, with elegantly set tables like those in an English tea shop. In addition to the typical pots of tea, unfortunately in bags not brewed, there are finger sandwiches, scones, and what American call cookies and British call biscuits. There is also a speaker who reminds us why we celebrate Christmas. Gatherings, like the Christmas Tea, are significantly important because these focus on Christ.

The tea is usually held at the beginning of the month. I surmise that is because women become super busy as the month goes on, but I would like to think it is intentional to help us focus on Christ. Starting the holiday on the right foot can help us focus on what is most important. Since so much demands our attention at Christmas, we need to be sure to make time for the things that matter.

There is always music at the tea and the ladies love to join voices and sing the "carols" of Christmas. Christmas songs are fun, but the carols remind us of that Holy Night when Christ was born. When singing carols, we join the herald angels in proclaiming God's great love for us. We sing of a child born to us that silent night. Each Christmas, we come faithfully once again to Bethlehem, to welcome Immanuel who has come to be with us. The carols bring the message of Christmas.

When I think of Christmas music, I remember my Grandma Sheaffer. She had a beautiful voice and even sang on the radio with her sisters. I think of them as the Harrisburg, PA version of The Andrew Sisters. Grandma's solo every Christmas Cantata was *O Holy Night*. I listen to that carol each year and remember her voice singing praise to God. She loved the Lord and she loved to sing the carols of Christmas. Her tradition on Christmas Eve was to play her 33 LP Christmas albums into the early morning hours as she rejoiced once again in the birth of her Savior.

During the pandemic, we were encouraged either to wear a face mask while singing, or not to sing at all. That was not easy. We need the freedom to sing loudly and proudly about what God has done for us. Christmas declares the marvelous work of God. It declares that, in Christ, God became man to dwell among us. Christ became a man to teach us how to best love God and one another. Then because we cannot save ourselves, Christ suffered death on a cross to pay for our sins. He arose victorious over death and conquered that for us all. How marvelous is this work of God!

Psalm 96:1–3 tells us:

> "¹*Oh sing to the* Lord *a new song;*
> *sing to the* Lord, *all the earth!*
> ²*Sing to the* Lord, *bless his name;*
> *tell of his salvation from day to day.*
> ³*Declare his glory among the nations,*
> *his marvelous works among all the peoples!*"

So sing this Christmas. My favorite Christmas CD features James Taylor singing, *Go Tell it on the Mountain.* I love to bellow that song with him. However, somehow I fall short of doing what the song says. I fail to proclaim, everywhere, that Jesus Christ is born. Now is a good time to proclaim from the mountains that Jesus Christ is born. Sing His praise. Fill your house with music proclaiming the birth of our Lord. Follow the instructions that Paul gave us in **Colossians 3:16,**

> *"Let the word of Christ dwell in you richly, teaching and admonishing one another in all wisdom, singing psalms and hymns and spiritual songs, with thankfulness in your hearts to God."*

Read: Ephesians 5:15–20

* ❋ What role does music play in your spiritual life?
* ❋ How can you use psalms, songs, and hymns to encourage others this Christmas?

Reflect: Sing. Play music. Share your favorite carols on social media or email the words to a friend. Send holiday greetings with the words of your favorite carols to others.

"Traditions! Traditions!"
December 12

*I*f I had to choose the most essential gathering at Christmas, it would be the Christmas Eve Service. It is difficult to imagine Christmas without it. That was not always the case for me, as my birth family did not attend a service on Christmas Eve. Our church did not have one. Instead, the Progress Church of God held a Cantata earlier in the month that was in many ways similar to the traditional Christmas Eve event. I have fond memories of those services. My whole family sang in the choir and all the choirs, children, youth, and adult, were gowned and held candles as they progressed into the sanctuary. One year my long red curls were singed by the flame of the child behind me, so after that, they changed to battery operated tapers. Otherwise, the service did not vary. It was the same songs and message every year, and it was at this service that my grandmother sang her *O Holy Night* solo. We liked that at Progress; it was our tradition.

As a teen, I started attending midnight services, at the Penbrook Lutheran Church, with my talented grandmother. Grandma had a tradition, as we left the service, of protectively carrying her lighted candle as we walked the several blocks to her home. She liked to light her bayberry candle from that flame. Grandma would keep the bayberry lit through the night, burning slowly, sitting in her sink to reduce the chance of a fire. I have tried to copy that tradition, but my son, Mark, successfully extinguishes the candle each year before we leave the sanctuary. That has become his tradition.

We all have special memories we associate with Christmas Eve and we establish traditions to pass those memories to new generations. However, circumstances change and alter the ways we can celebrate. We experienced that in 2020, when many Christmas Eve services were cancelled or became virtual online gatherings. It is at these times that we must remember that the event itself is not important, but celebrating the birth of Christ is. No matter how you celebrate Christmas Eve this year, know **Philippians 2:6–8**, is still true:

> "⁶*who, though he was in the form of God, did not count equality with God a thing to be grasped,* ⁷*but emptied himself, by taking the form of a servant, being born in the likeness of men.* ⁸*And being found in human form, he humbled himself by becoming obedient to the point of death, even death on a cross.*"

Christmas Eve is the night we remember and celebrate the birth of God as a man. God, limiting Himself in ways we cannot comprehend, in order to provide salvation for a sinful people. This is the message of the holiday. This is what we celebrate and nothing in the world can change that fact. Despite the situation we may find ourselves in on Christmas Eve, we need to focus on Christ. We cannot let our man-created traditions get in our way. Traditions are good, however, we are not celebrating the tradition; we are celebrating Christ who gave up much that we might gain life. Christ who existed from before the creation of the earth, yet entered His creation as a man to reveal the glory of our Father.

John 1:1, 14 reminds us of Christ's role in creation and our lives.

> "¹*In the beginning was the Word, and the Word was with God, and the Word was God.*"

> "¹⁴*And the Word became flesh and dwelt among us, and we have seen his glory, glory as of the only Son from the Father, full of grace and truth.*"

Read: Philippians 2:6–8

❈ How is Jesus both God and man?

❈ In what ways did Jesus humble Himself to become man?

Reflect: Plan now for your Christmas Eve. Hopefully you can attend a traditional service, but if circumstances prevent that this year, plan how you can celebrate Christmas Eve meaningfully wherever you are. Let your focus be on Christ. Look beyond the secular trappings of Christmas Eve and anticipate the coming of our Savior. Perhaps you can have candles ready to light as you sing, *Silent Night*. Ask others to participate by reading Scripture or a devotional. If need be, meet on Zoom. Try a "Google" search for Christmas Eve services and you may find one that will meet your family's needs.

Week Three
"GAIETY"

Susan Weber

GAIETY

*C*hristmas is the most wonderful time of the year. Most people are happy at Christmas. There are so many things to look forward to and to participate in. Everything is decorated, people wear festive clothing, and there are delicious treats surrounding us. In fact, the gaiety of Christmas has started to overshadow the real reason for the season. Secular signs of the holiday greatly out number spiritual ones.

I think one of the positive effects of the Covid-19 pandemic was that it gave me time to rethink how I celebrate Christmas. Since I wasn't as busy, overwhelmed, or surrounded with the world's message as in times past, I had a chance to pause and consider how I could best celebrate Christ's birth without the typical festivities that demanded my attention. I couldn't go as many places and people weren't coming to my house so that limited my need and desire to decorate and bake. I had a chance to rethink how I celebrated and what was really important.

This wasn't the first time I considered how I celebrated Christmas. Several years ago I decided to be more intentional about this holiday celebration. I started thinking about the objects I used to decorate my house and I was inspired to decorate with nativities, instead of Santas. I wanted my house to reflect the spiritual, and not the secular focus of Christmas. Seriously, should that even be a thing — a secular Christmas?

In 2020, I made more changes to focus my celebration on Christ and guard myself from the cultural trappings of the holiday. I think this needs to be a yearly exercise as it is easy to be caught up in society's view of the event. My goal is to keep Christ in the center of my celebration.

One cautionary note as we prepare for Christmas is to remember that there are those who are suffering, those who are mourning, and those who have not embraced the hope that was born at Christmas. May we, in our gaiety, be aware of those who are not joyfully celebrating.

"Gaiety or Great Joy?"
December 13

*I*n the third week of Advent, the church lights the Shepherd's candle, or the candle of joy. I think of this as my candle since my maiden name was Sheaffer, which is German for shepherd. Therefore, these verses from **Luke 2:8–12** resonate with me:

> "⁸*And in the same region there were shepherds out in the field, keeping watch over their flock by night.* ⁹*And an angel of the Lord appeared to them, and the glory of the Lord shone around them, and they were filled with great fear.* ¹⁰*And the angel said to them, "Fear not, for behold, I bring you good news of* **GREAT JOY** *that will be for all the people.* ¹¹*For unto you is born this day in the city of David a Savior, who is Christ the Lord.* ¹²*And this will be a sign for you: you will find a baby wrapped in swaddling cloths and lying in a manger."*

The birth of Christ was a cause for great joy two thousand years ago, and it is a cause for great joy today. The world pandemic of 2020 brought many disappointments. Lives were lost, milestone events were ruined, jobs disappeared, school terms were disrupted, vacations were postponed, and many of our plans were affected. However, despite all these disappointments and sorrows, the news of Christ's birth is still a cause for joy.

It is easy to focus on our losses and become depressed. Life is hard and has many challenges. Each year can bring more sorrow. Christmas also falls in December when winter is approaching and the days are getting shorter and the nights are colder. The increasing hours of darkness and coldness add to our feelings of isolation and loneliness.

With this in mind, consider the lot of the shepherds. Shepherds have isolated, lonely work as they guard the sheep during the watches of the night. They need to stay alert and be willing to fight off wild animals and other dangers that may threaten the flock. Interestingly, God chose to send angels to these watchmen to announce the birth of His Son. The shepherds were the first to receive God's message of great joy. They responded accordingly, following the angels instructions, rejoicing. Just as the shepherds did, we too, need to rise above our circumstances and respond each Christmas with joy.

So instead of focusing on what we lost this year, let us focus on the great joy we were given. Focus on this Good News proclaimed by the angels. Put aside your feelings of loss and disappointment, and be renewed by the story of our Savior's birth.

Luke 1:14

*"And you will have **joy** and gladness, and many will rejoice at His birth,"*

Read: Luke 2:8–12

* What worries might the shepherds have put aside to receive the joy of Christ?
* What do you need to set aside to receive the joy of Christ this Christmas?

Reflect: Wrap your worldly concerns in prayer and ask God to fill you with His joy this Christmas. Play your favorite Christmas carols. Put on your favorite Christmas sweater. Make your favorite Christmas treat. Share the joy with a friend or neighbor. Spread the joy.

Consider, also, someone who may need their "joy" tank filled. Include them in your holiday preparations. Do not just take them cookies, but invite them to bake treats with you. Give them opportunities to be participants in creating the joy, and not only be passive receivers of your gifts.

"Let your CHRISTMAS Lights Shine"
December 14

I tend to play more music on the radio in December than in any other month. Currently, my radio is blaring, "It's the Most Wonderful Time of the Year". I agree with that sentiment, but not for the reasons listed in this tune. The song's inventory suggests that jingle bells, good cheer, marshmallows, mistletoe, parties, ghost stories, and tales from long ago, are the reason this season is so wonderful. But I noticed the most essential element is missing, unless you count the good news of our Savior as a tale from long, long ago, there is no mention of Christ.

The gaiety of Christmas is expressed in many ways, but few point to the Savior's birth. We plan parties, decorate, wear Christmas sweaters, send holiday greetings, and prepare special foods. These are ways we express the joy of the holiday in our culture. All of these are synonymous with Christmas, however, many of these traditions have no real connection to the Biblical account of Christ's birth. Nor do these things focus us on Christ.

In 2020, when our ability to celebrate was limited by the pandemic, we had an opportunity to reflect on how we celebrate and how we might refocus our celebration on the real source of joy, the birth of Jesus. Perhaps, like cleaning out a closet, we should do that every year. We need to sweep out the Christmas traditions that do not focus on Christ and focus on the ones that do.

I am thinking of outdoor decorations today. Many of us place candles in our windows and decorate our bushes and trees with holiday lights and lawn ornaments. Lights are an appropriate symbol of Christ, as recorded in **John 8:12** – *"Again Jesus spoke to them, saying, 'I am the light of the world. Whoever follows me will not walk in darkness, but will have the light of life."* **John 1:4–5** says, *"4 In him was life, and the life was the light of men. 5 The light shines in the darkness, and the darkness has not overcome it."*

Jesus came to shine light into the darkness of the world. The world is dark with sin, but Christ shines His light into that darkness that we might have life. That is the illuminating message of Christmas. Yet, as I cruise my neighborhood, lawns are filled with giant inflatable Santas, Rudolphs, and even dragons with Santa stocking caps. Perhaps this Christmas is the year we abandon lawn ornaments that are secular and focus on the manger and the light that was born to us on Christmas. May we proclaim Christ, Who is the light of the world.

Isaiah 9:2

*"The people who walked in darkness have seen a great **light**; those who dwelt in a land of deep darkness, on them has **light** shone."*

Read: Matthew 5:14–15

❊ Christ is the light of the world, but He has charged us to be light also. How can you show Christ's light this Christmas?

✻ In what ways is your light under a bushel? How can you reveal it?

Reflect: Consider how you can decorate the entrance to your home to invite others to see the light of Christ this year. At my house, my husband and I usually put up a few strands of lights around the shrubbery. We would not win any light display contest! In 2020, we evaluated our outdoor display and chose to add a crèche. We wanted to make the statement that at our house we celebrate the birth of Christ.

"Mixed Messages"
December 15

*Y*esterday we talked about our outdoor decorations. Today I would like to consider our indoor ones. We love to decorate our homes and there are even television stations dedicated to showing us new and better ways to do so. One of my favorite places to get holiday ideas is at the annual *Four Lanes End Garden Club Holiday House Tour* held on the Thursday before Thanksgiving. Several homes in the community are chosen to be decorated around a holiday theme. The ladies spend months creating their displays and people come from all over the county to view the homes and gather ideas. People love to find new ways to provide gaiety in their homes for the holiday.

I saw an interesting display when I visited the Holy Land during December in 2013. We visited the synagogue in Nazareth where Jesus worshipped as a child. It is now a church. They had a manager scene near their altar, but instead of a star atop the stable, there was a Santa Claus. Wow, that was a mixed message!

What mixed message do we send when we place Santa more prominently in our homes than we do Christ? Please do not misunderstand. I have nothing against St. Nick, but the holiday is not about him. It is about Christ. Which decorations do you think please God? We read in **Ephesians 5:8–10,**

> "⁸*for at one time you were darkness, but now you are light in the Lord. Walk as children of light ⁹(for the fruit of light is found in all that is good and right and true), ¹⁰and try to discern what is pleasing to the Lord.*"

As children of light, how do we present that light to others and please the Lord?

As a child, Santa was an important part of Christmas, and although I was a believer, the secular parts of Christmas appealed to me. As an adult, I am still surrounded by the secular signs of the season everywhere I go. I cannot choose what is displayed in a store, my office, or any other place I visit. There have been court cases challenging the legality of displaying Nativity scenes on public property. I may not be able to choose what is displayed in public, however, I can choose what is presented in my home. I would like to surround my family and visitors with symbols of the Biblical account of Christmas. Those symbols include light, angels, stars and nativities. We have many choices. Think of symbols that proclaim the Lord and are good, right and true. I am sure it will please Him.

Philippians 4:8 tells us,

> "*Finally, brothers, whatever is true, whatever is honorable, whatever is just, whatever is pure, whatever is lovely, whatever is commendable, if there is any excellence, if there is anything worthy of praise, think about these things…*"

What are the true, honorable, just, pure, lovely, commendable, excellent things that we should use in our homes at Christmas? Do you include those in your decorating?

Read: Proverbs 3:1–4

* ❋ How can you write God's love and faithfulness on your heart?
* ❋ How can you keep God's love before yourself throughout this Christmas season?

Reflect: Think about your Christmas decorations. How can you focus your displays on Christ and not secular expressions of the season? Think of things that will focus those in your home on the Lord. I have a friend who collects nativities. What a wonderful reminder of Christ's birth to see her display from different countries and different time periods. It is encouraging to be reminded that people in the past and all over the world celebrate the birth of our Savior.

"Food for Thought"
December 16

What is a celebration without food? Food certainly has a special place in Christmas preparation.

There are books dedicated to helping you arrange for the best holiday feasts ever. Preparing these treats is also a special part of the celebration. I am sure we all have wonderful memories of rolling dough, cutting out shapes, and decorating sugar cookies or helping to stuff a turkey, or mold butter into a holiday shape. I like to use holiday shaped cookie cutters to create treats from the canned cranberry sauce.

Every house has their favorite Christmas goodies. I loved my Grandmother Lloyd's chocolate cutouts and my Grandma Sheaffer's sugar cookies with creamy icing. My mom made the best sand tarts, and my mother-in-law made *Jumbles* with raisins or coconut. Is your mouth watering? I am sure you are now envisioning your favorite Christmas treat.

Besides cookies, there are the holiday feasts. When I was a child, it was a Christmas Day turkey dinner, which was exactly like Thanksgiving, but somehow better because it included presents. I now celebrate my family Christmas feast on Christmas Eve, and our new tradition is beef tenderloin. One year we had a military family, whose Dad was on a deployment, visit on Christmas Day. We asked them to bring their favorite Christmas treat and it was hot fudge sundaes for dessert. That was a first for us and a very sweet memory.

Preparing the Christmas treats take a lot of time. That includes planning, shopping, and creating the dish. Even if we take advantage of the many restaurants and bakeries that are willing to do it for us, we still need to plan, order, and pick up. Due to the pandemic in 2020, we suddenly did not need to prepare feasts or treats. We were limited in our gathering and, therefore, had no need for all the food items for these events. So what did you do with that extra time? I found that I could use that extra time to prepare my mind for Christmas. I exchanged my baking time for meditating time. With nowhere I could rush to, or no one to bake for, I had time to think more about God and Christmas.

Did you find yourself with extra time during the pandemic? What did you fill that with? The pandemic gave many of us extra time to develop new habits, and a habit of meditating on God's Word is an excellent one. In fact, the New Year is only two weeks away so why not take this time to jumpstart a New Year's resolution and make daily meditation part of your routine?

Psalms 119:7–8 says,

> *"7I will praise You with an upright heart,*
> *when I learn Your righteous rules.*
> *8I will keep Your statutes;*
> *do not utterly forsake me!"*

In this verse, the psalmist pledges to do three things: praise God, learn His rules, and keep them. Taking some of the extra "Christmas prep" time to prepare your heart for the New Year may be what you need to be ready for the challenges ahead. So bake a small batch of cookies, grab one and a cup of coffee or tea. Snuggle into a comfy chair and open up God's Word—He has prepared many goodies for you there!

Psalm 34:8ₐ

*"Oh, **taste and see** that the Lord is good!"*

Read: Psalm 119:1–8

* ❋ What would you have to do to seek the Lord with your whole heart?
* ❋ Have you been steadfast in keeping His statutes?

Reflect: Carve out time to spend more time with Christ this Christmas season. If you like giving home baked goods to friends and neighbors, how can you share Christ with them this year? I am considering a Christmas cactus for my neighbors. I love when they bloom at Christmas and Easter.

"Send the Right Message"
December 17

During the recent pandemic, one Christmas tradition that was not impacted by being socially distant was sending Christmas greetings. In fact, this tradition was even more needed as it was an opportunity to encourage others during a difficult time. Traditionally the Christmas card brought a remembrance of the holiday and was filled with good wishes for the recipient. However, recently our culture has moved away from the classic Christmas card to a note with a family portrait and a long letter giving an account of the past year. These Christmas greetings help people to stay in touch, but I am wondering if they help people to celebrate the joy of Christmas.

Although it is nice to share what is happening in your life, sometimes that news may fall on ears that are struggling and are having difficulty rejoicing with you. The recipient may have a need to be encouraged this holiday season and the message may discourage them, even though that was not the intent. Some hearts need to be lifted, they may be so burdened that they cannot see past their despair to see your joy.

Paul gives us good examples for greeting others in his New Testament letters. Look at this greeting from Paul and Timothy's letter to the **Philippians 1:1–3,**

> "¹*Paul and Timothy, servants of Christ Jesus,*
>
> *To all the saints in Christ Jesus who are at Philippi, with the overseers and deacons:*
>
> ²*'Grace to you and peace from God our Father and the Lord Jesus Christ.*
>
> ³*I thank my God in all my remembrance of you,* **always** *in every prayer of mine for you all making my prayer with joy, because of your partnership in the gospel from the first day until now. And I am sure of this, that he who began a good work in you will bring it to completion at the day of Jesus Christ."*

Notice what Paul included in his greeting. He notes who is writing the letter, Paul and Timothy, and that they are servants of Christ. Then he identifies the recipients: the believers in Philippi. He sends them grace and peace from God. Finally, he thanks God for all He is doing in the lives. Interestingly, the greeting is more about the recipient than the sender, whereas, our current holiday cards tend to be more about the sender than the recipient.

What if this year, we made our greetings about the recipient and affirm what the Lord is doing in their lives? What if our greeting expressed thankfulness for how the Lord is using them? This would take us back to the days before we could mass print our letters, a time when we hand wrote individualized notes instead. That is a lot of work, but maybe it is worth the time. It would also encourage our fellow believers, and we have been asked by God to do this.

In **1 Thessalonians 5:11** we read,

"Therefore encourage one another and build one another up, just as you are doing." Think about this today. How can you encourage others this Christmas when sending your Christmas greeting? What recognition in their lives would make their day? Consider scripture that you can include that might enhance the recipient's life. Bless them with God's Word and encouragement from you.

Read: Romans 16:1–17

- ❋ What do you learn from these personal greetings?
- ❋ How might you encourage others in their walk of faith in your cards this year?

Reflect: Focus on the receiver as you write your cards this year. Choose greetings this year that focus on Christ. Think of ways to encourage others in their walk with the Lord. Tell them how their friendship is a gift to you.

"Spread JOY"
December 18

⸎

There is a difference between gaiety and joy. That difference is evident in how the world celebrates the holiday season and how it was intended. Our culture has made Christmas a season of happiness, but God intended it as a season of great joy.

In **Matthew 2:10**, the magi see Christ's star and their reaction is great joy. *"When they saw the star, they rejoiced exceedingly with great joy."* And the angel's announcement in **Luke 2: 10** says, *"Fear not, for behold, I bring you good news of great joy that will be for all the people."* The response to the birth of Christ is joy. The promise of Christmas is the birth of a Savior. No other news could bring this great joy.

However, the world has changed Christmas to focus on happiness and gaiety, and as a result we miss the great joy. There is nothing wrong with happiness and gaiety, but they depend on the situation and circumstances, and great joy does not. We can have great joy this Christmas despite a virus, loss of income, poor health, or loss of loved ones. Independent of our circumstances we can rejoice in the hope found in the birth of a Savior. He is the One who came to save the world from their sins and will reconcile them with God to live with Him forever.

In the Christmas story, we see examples of people who overcome their circumstances to receive the joy of Christ's birth. Look at Mary and Joseph's situation. In Mary's ninth month of pregnancy, she had to travel 90 miles from her home by decree of the government and it was 90 miles uphill. Pregnancy was not an exemption and she gave birth in a borrowed stable without the support of her female family members. To make matters worse, soon after Jesus was born, Mary and Joseph had to flee Herod's edict to kill male children under the age of two. They became refugees in a foreign land. Their situation was very difficult and yet they embraced the great joy in the birth of a son whose birth was announced by angels as the coming of a Savior. They trusted God and not their situation.

The shepherds also did not have the best circumstances. They had one of the lowliest, most difficult professions. They spent nights outdoors on the hillside and risked their lives to protect the sheep. Yet, they were chosen by God to be the first to hear of the Savior's birth. They also looked beyond their situation and went to the stable and worshipped the baby, and embraced the great joy.

Perhaps you are not cheerful this Christmas. Perhaps your situation this year is crushing your spirit and you are not happy. However, you can still share the great joy. Do not let your circumstances deny you the great joy found in the good news that Christ is born.

In **I John 4:14** we read,

> *"And we have seen and testify that the Father has sent his Son to be the Savior of the world."*

Do not allow yourself to lose the opportunity to be joyful this year. Do not value worldly happiness over the eternal joy found in Christ. In our society, this is not an easy thing to do. The world's messages constantly encourages us to pursue our individual happiness and promotes our entitlement to be happy. God, however, isn't offering you happiness, He is giving you joy that is found in the hope of Christ. Don't settle for temporal happiness, when you can receive eternal joy.

Read: Matthew 28:7–9

* ❋ Why were the women filled with great joy?
* ❋ Are you filled with great joy this Christmas?

Reflect: How can you share the great joy of our Savior's birth? It is one thing to spread happiness during this season, but a greater blessing to all is to spread the great joy of knowing Christ.

Week Four
"GOD WITH US"

Sheryl Vasso

GOD WITH US

*D*id you know that it is God's desire to be with you? It may be difficult to realize this because it seems too good to be true. However, what the almighty and powerful Creator wants is to be with us! This is the theme of the Bible: God created us, He loves us, sin **separated** and **distanced** us from Him, and then God brought us **spiritually close** again through His beloved Son, Jesus Christ!

> *"The LORD is near to all who call on him,*
> *to all who call on him in truth."*

Psalm 145:18

During this final week of Advent, we are going to consider various aspects of what it really means that **God is with Us**. So many people are living life without all God came to give, and my prayer is that you are not one of them. May you walk in greater fullness of His presence and purpose!

*Father, thank You for **GIVING** your Son, Jesus, to be with us. Thank You that you did not stay distant, but You*

*left the magnificence of Heaven to come to Earth to rescue and **GATHER** us close to Yourself again. Holy Spirit, teach us what it fully means that You are with us. Give us the joy and **GAIETY** of the promise of **GOD with US!***

"I Love a Good Preposition"
December 19

"Behold, the virgin shall conceive and bear a son,
and they shall call his name Immanuel"

(Matthew 1:23)

*T*he year 2020 reminded me of how much I love a good preposition!
For sure it was a very difficult year and probably no one needs
to be reminded of that. The world experienced great difficulty from a
global pandemic, to national protests, and toilet paper supply panic!

As a result, many may have questioned, "Where was God?"

The answer to that question is found in **Matthew 1:23**, and it is a
comforting answer for every year, not just 2020. This verse declares a
great truth that brought a soothing assurance to Joseph when he first
heard it on the heels of the difficult news that his fiancée, Mary, was
pregnant. It also encouraged the faithful, on that first Christmas, as
they waited for God to speak up after four hundred years of silence.
And it has been an encouragement to believers ever since!

I was not always excited, as an elementary student, to sing the song about the 48 prepositions. Do you remember those little terms that expressed the relationship between one word and another? For example, "The birds flew *above* my head, *around* my head, *below* my head." However, the longer I read the Word of God, the more I have come to appreciate the grammar lessons of my early school days, especially the grammar lessons about prepositions. In **Matthew 1:23** there is a preposition we should all get excited about every Christmas because it brings a comforting perspective to our difficult seasons. The preposition "with" answers our question, "Where was God?" In our times of great difficulty, God is "**with**" us. He is not "against" us, away "from" us, or "beyond" us. Rather, every Christmas, no matter the year, we are reminded that God is "**with**" us.

It is interesting to note that Matthew stresses that God is with us in the beginning of his Gospel (**1:23**) and again at the end of his gospel in **Matthew 28:20.** It feels like a huge hug from our Heavenly Father.

*"And behold, I am **with** you always, to the end of the age."*

Do you see why I love a good preposition? Who would have thought that a tiny part of speech could bring such comfort to Joseph long ago, and to us now? Where was God in 2020 or in any dark year we may have experienced before or since? He was and is "**with**" us!

Read: Matthew 1 and Matthew 28

Reflect: What is it about difficult times that makes us question where God is? What practical things can you do to remind yourself that God is always *with* you?

"God with All Nations"
December 20

"*¹Now after Jesus was born in Bethlehem of Judea in the days of Herod the king, behold, magi from the east arrived in Jerusalem, saying, ²'Where is he who has been born king of the Jews? For we saw His star in the east and have come to worship Him.'*"

Matthew 2:1–2 (NASB)

Unlike Luke's gospel, Matthew's gospel does not tell about the shepherds coming to visit Jesus in the stable. Matthew's focus is on the magi coming from the East to worship Jesus. We often refer to these magi as the "three wise men", or "three kings", who brought the new "born king of the Jews", gifts of gold, frankincense and myrrh. How many wise men, and how old Jesus was when the wise men arrived, are not clear from Matthew's account. However, what we do know is that the men from the East were magi, or astrologers who gained an international reputation for astrology, a highly regarded science at that time.

It makes sense, therefore, that God would use a star to guide the magi to Jesus. God knew how to get their attention! While many theories exist about the ethnicity and background of these men from the East, perhaps from Babylon, one thing we know for sure is that they were not Jews. They were Gentiles. Unclean. Foreigners.

Matthew, both at the beginning of his Gospel, and at the end, portrays Jesus as a universal Messiah for the nations, not just for Jews! In the beginning of Matthew's Gospel, we read:

> [23] *"Behold, the virgin shall conceive and bear a son, and they shall call his name Immanuel" (which means, God with us).*

Matthew 1:23

And at the end of Matthew's Gospel, the last words of Jesus are:

> *"[18] And Jesus came and said to them, 'All authority in heaven and on earth has been given to me. [19] Go therefore and make disciples of all nations, baptizing them in the name of the Father and of the Son and of the Holy Spirit, [20] teaching them to observe all that I have commanded you. And behold, I am with you always, to the end of the age.'"*

Matthew 28:18–20

This is consistent with one of the repeated prophecies that the nations and kings would come to Jesus as the ruler of the world. For example, **Isaiah 60:3** reads,

> *"Nations will come to your light,*
> *and kings to the brightness of your rising."*

While Jesus was born with a pure Jewish lineage, and certainly came to redeem the ones He had chosen from the start, He also came to bring ALL people back into relationship with their Creator. He reduced the distance between and drew us spiritually close!

Anyone who has faith in Jesus has become a chosen child of God. Jesus' heart is for the world and He desires all nations to know Him. Jesus' heart is for the world to draw spiritually close to Him!

Read: Matthew 2:1–12; John 3:16

Reflect: What did Herod request of the wise men after they had found Christ in Bethlehem? What did the wise men do and why? (Matthew 2)

For whom did Jesus die? (John 3:16)
How have you experienced *Immanuel* — God being with you, in your life thus far?

"The Vast Sum of Them"
December 21

❦

"The weather is here. Wish you were beautiful." This is my classic line on any postcard I send to family or friends while I am a great distance from them. Somewhere on the three-inch space on the back of a postcard, I will pen these words. It is expected. However, in my playfulness, my loved ones know that although distance separates us, I am thinking of them. My mom will say to me, before I leave on a trip, "You'll be too busy to think of me." However, I always respond, "Of course I'll think of you. You are in my heart!" And while this is true, and while I do daily think of her and many others, I am sure I fall short of the vast sum of the thoughts that God has towards us.

We read in **Psalm 139:17–18**,

"¹⁷How precious to me are your thoughts, O God!
How vast is the sum of them!
¹⁸If I would count them, they are more than the sand.
I awake, and I am still with you."

David marveled about the preciousness of God's thoughts toward him and the VAST amount of those thoughts. The psalmist was always on God's mind and he knew that God was always with him and knew him so well. Just as David mattered to God, we also matter to God. He knows us infinitely and has countless thoughts about us. He understands and cares for us beyond our understanding. God has eliminated all distancing between Him and us!

It may be challenging at times, especially during a pandemic when we purposefully distance ourselves from others, to imagine that we are never more than a thought away from God's mind. Yet, God assures us that He has a vast sum of thoughts about us. He assures us that He will not forget us by engraving us on the palm of His hands.

> "¹⁵Can a woman forget her nursing child,
> that she should have no compassion on the son
> of her womb?
> Even these may forget,
> yet I will not forget you.
> ¹⁶Behold, I have engraved you on the palms of my hands;
> your walls are continually before me."

> **Isaiah 49:15–16**

It is unlikely that a woman, nursing her child, could possibly forget that child. However, God is saying that even if this unlikely occurrence were to happen, He will never forget us!

In my finite thoughts about God, I think of Him as being very busy. I cannot fathom, just as my Mom could not fathom about me, that He has time to think about ME and the other 7 billion people in the world. Yet, He tells us in this Psalm that He not only thinks of us, but His thoughts about us are infinite and eternal. His thoughts and remembrance of us are more than the sand!

Even after a night's sleep, or a nap on the innumerable granules of sand on the beach, we are still with Him, and He with us. We never have to wish He were here, beautiful weather or not!

Read: Romans 8:38–39; Philippians 2:13

Reflect: Do you sometimes struggle with believing God is with you? Why or why not? What is one way you can remind yourself that God is with you?

"A Standing Invitation"
December 22

*There is something about an invitation which makes us feel accepted, wanted, special, and included. Having a *standing invitation* makes us feel even more accepted, wanted, special, and included. A standing invitation means we are always welcome and invited to visit at any time.

Invitations are powerful, both in this life, and in the Bible. In **Esther 4**, we learn that Queen Esther received a copy of the decree to exterminate the Jews, and her cousin, Mordecai, challenged her to intercede on behalf of her people before the king. Esther explained the difficulty behind Mordecai's prompting:

> *"All the king's servants and the people of the king's provinces know that if any man or woman goes to the king inside the inner court without being called, there is but one law—to be put to death, except the one to whom the king holds out the golden scepter so that he may live. But as for me, I have not been called to come in to the king these thirty days."* (**Esther 4:11**)

The only confidence Esther had about going before the king, without an invitation, was that she was breaking the "one law" which could result in her death! Esther did not have a standing invitation to come before the king.

However, as we read further in chapter 4, Esther determined to go before the king without his bidding, and with great courage she declared, "*If I perish, I perish*" (**4:16**). I can only imagine what she wondered as she stood before the king. Would the king hold out his scepter and grant her approach? Would she live to see another sunrise?

What a comfort it is for us to know that we have a *standing invitation* with the King of Kings! Unlike Esther, who could not approach her king, we may approach our King with surety.

> "Let us then with confidence draw near to the throne of grace, that we may receive mercy and find grace to help in time of need."

> **Hebrews 4:16**

It is probably accurate to say that the global pandemic of 2020, eliminated any standing invitations we may have had with our friends and loved ones. Feeling free to visit at any time was replaced with social distancing. I know that I was very careful about whom I allowed to enter my home and about entering other people's homes. However, what a wonderful confidence we have, that nothing, not even a global pandemic, can nullify our standing invitation to be spiritually close to God. Not only may we confidently approach the King without fear of death, or fear of spreading or contracting a virus, but we may be confident to receive mercy (*not getting* what we deserve) and find grace (*getting* what we do not deserve) to help in our **time of need**! God wants us to come into His courts; He desires for us to draw close to Him and to not stand at a distance!

Thankfully, God provides help in our time of need and no request is too small, because He wants us to *"...let your requests be made known to God."* (**Philippians 4:6**).

There is something about an invitation that makes us feel accepted, wanted, special, and included. Having a *standing invitation* makes us feel even more accepted, wanted, special, and included because a standing invitation from someone, means we are always welcome and we are always invited to visit at any time! We are always welcome to draw near to the throne of grace with the confidence that our Father wants to help in our time of need!

Read: Esther 4

Reflect: What must it have been like to be Esther and not know if her husband, the king, would grant her access to his throne? How courageous she must have been to approach him without an invitation! Fortunately, unlike Esther with her king, we have a standing invitation with our King who desires to be with us! How are you taking advantage of that invitation? Are there times you refrain from approaching Him? Why or why not?

"What do you want for Christmas?"
December 23

One of the most asked questions during the Christmas season is, "What do you want for Christmas?" My pat answer has always been "peace on earth" and, more often than not, I have received a glass globe ornament with a world map and the word "peace" etched on it. Those gifts were creative responses to my request, and admittedly, a world peace ornament was the best that anyone could do within their power to grant peace on earth. Peace on earth is something most of us have yet to experience in our lifetime.

It has always fascinated me to read about the series of Christmas truce ceasefires that took place around Christmas 1914, during the First World War. Supposedly on Christmas Eve and Christmas Day, German and British soldiers tore down their boundaries and mingled and exchanged food and gifts and some even played a game of football or two. In more recent times of war, it is not unusual to hear of, maybe not a gift exchange, but at least a ceasefire on Christmas Day. Part of my fascination is that it causes me to wonder what could extend a truce, a moment of peace and humanity during the atrocity of war, into something more lasting.

In Isaiah's prophesy about the coming Messiah, he says,

> *"For to us a child is born, to us a son is given;*
> *and the government shall be upon His shoulder,*
> *and His name shall be called*
> *Wonderful Counselor, Mighty God,*
> *Everlasting Father, Prince of Peace."*

Isaiah 9:6

In a world filled with global pandemics, war, violence, financial chaos, and broken relationships, it may be difficult to see how the infant Jesus could be the all-powerful peaceful God. However, physical safety and political harmony do not necessarily reflect the kind of peace that describes Jesus. The kind of peace that Jesus offers is so much more than the absence of war, and so much longer than one single day.

The Hebrew word for peace, "shalom", is often used in reference to calm and tranquility. But the deeper meaning of peace has to do with being restored with God. Jesus came to reconcile us to God, to bring peace between God and man by becoming the sacrificial lamb for our sins.

In our sinful state, we are enemies with God,

> *"For if while we were enemies we were reconciled to God*
> *by the death of his Son, much more, now that we are rec-*
> *onciled, shall we be saved by his life."*

Romans 5:10

SOCIALLY DISTANT, SPIRITUALLY CLOSE | 81

"…but God shows his love for us in that while we were still sinners, Christ died for us.

Romans 5:8

Because of Christ's sacrifice, we are restored to a relationship of peace with God. **Romans 5:1** reads,

"Therefore, since we have been justified by faith, we have peace with God through our Lord Jesus Christ."

This is the deep, abiding peace between our hearts and our Creator that cannot be taken away. It is the ultimate fulfillment of Christ's work as "Prince of Peace."

I am writing this while sitting in front of my Christmas tree staring at a peace on earth ornament. B101 radio is playing, *Silent Night*, while outside the hustle and bustle of last minute shopping is in full force. As I listen to the words of the carol, I am reminded that I still want peace for Christmas…peace on earth yes, but more than that, I want peace in my heart.

What do *you* want for Christmas? Why not ask the Prince of Peace, the Holy Infant, wrapped not in shiny paper, but in swaddling rags of humanity, to lay His head in the straw of your heart? He is the Mighty God who has the power to offer peace that is not just a Christmas truce ceasefire for today, but an everlasting, heavenly peace.

"Peace I leave with you; my peace I give to you. Not as the world gives do I give to you. Let not your hearts be troubled, neither let them be afraid."

John 14:27

Read: Romans 5; John 16:33; 2 Corinthians 5:18–20

Reflect: How do these verses of Scripture tell us we have reconciled, made peace, with God? What comfort do we find from our Lord as we live in a world full of tribulation? How should making peace with God translate into making peace with others?

"The Eve of Christmas"
December 24

Christmas Eve has long been my favorite day of the year. The anticipation of Christmas day, memories of my brothers and parents attending a church service at midnight, and then returning home to gather around our fireplace while each of us opened one gift, ate some cookies, and drank hot chocolate (with marshmallows of course). Those Christmas Eves are now serene memories of more peaceful times!

It is probably safe to say that 2020 was anything but peaceful, in all that surrounded us, and in all that was within our own hearts at times. It is also probably safe to say that 1968, 52 years before the pandemic, was also not very peaceful as the United States had experienced an extremely turbulent year. Robert F. Kennedy and Martin Luther King Jr. had been assassinated, the war in Vietnam had escalated, and race riots had broken out in many cities across the country.

However, there was one unifying event that brought together tens of thousands of spectators. That event was the launch of Apollo 8 on December 21, 1968. Three astronauts, Frank Borman, Jim Lovell Jr., and Bill Anders boarded a spacecraft which became the first manned flight to have ever left the Earth's gravitational field! On December 24, Christmas Eve, the astronauts became the first humans to see the dark side of the moon (I always thought that was just a dessert) and to circle it 10 times. They had also become the first to see the Earth, from a distance, as a whole planet (like a big blue marble in space).

The Apollo 8 crew had taken a TV camera into space and did six live broadcasts over the course of the mission. One of the six broadcasts was aired during prime time on Christmas Eve to an audience of one billion, or one out of every four people living on the planet at the time.

The astronauts were told that on Christmas Eve they would have the largest audience that had ever listened to a human voice, and the only instructions they received from NASA was to do something "appropriate". So the men pointed their camera out the window and filmed the moon's mountains, craters, and seas and then ended their broadcast by taking turns reading the first ten verses of Genesis 1. They said they selected this particular passage because it was the foundation of "many of the world's religions," and not just Christianity, and thus they deemed it "appropriate" to read. Of course, not everyone agreed with this reasoning and the well-known atheist, Madalyn Murray O'Hair, filed a lawsuit over the reading.

The years 2020 and 1968 may go down in history as years which lacked peace and were very turbulent. However, take heart, because Jesus grants peace unlike any peace the world or the universe can offer, and therefore we need not be afraid!

> "Peace I leave with you; my peace I give to you. Not as the world gives do I give to you. Let not your hearts be troubled, neither let them be afraid."

John 14:27

SOCIALLY DISTANT, SPIRITUALLY CLOSE | 85

Read: Genesis 1; Luke 2 (a great reading for Christmas Day)

Reflect: How will Christmas be different if you begin and end your day with the firm belief that God is with you? How would your life be different if you begin and end each day with the firm belief that God is with you?

"A FINAL WORD
IN ONE WORD"

If we were to sum up Christmas in one word, it would be "Immanuel" (God with us). The prophet, Isaiah, was the first to introduce us to this glorious name:

> *"Therefore the Lord himself will give you a sign. Behold,*
> *the virgin shall conceive and bear a son, and shall call*
> *His name Immanuel."*

Isaiah 7:14

We know, without any doubt, that this prophecy concerns Jesus Christ, because in the opening chapter of the New Testament, Matthew makes this connection,

> *"20But as he considered these things, behold, an angel of*
> *the Lord appeared to him in a dream, saying, "Joseph, son*
> *of David, do not fear to take Mary as your wife, for that*
> *which is conceived in her is from the Holy Spirit. 21She*

will bear a son, and you shall call his name Jesus, for
*He will save His people from their sins." *²³*All this took*
place to fulfill what the Lord had spoken by the prophet.
"Behold, the virgin shall conceive and bear a son, and they
shall call His name Immanuel."

Matthew 1:20–23

One of the most comforting names of Jesus is "Immanuel" which literally means, "God with us"! This title captures the mystery and the miracle that is Christmas. The Almighty God, who crafted the galaxies with His bare hands (**Genesis 1:1**), the Eternal Word, Who always was and always will be (**John 1:1**), came to Earth in the form of a help-less baby. Why? Because our sins made it impossible for us to come to Him. God took the extravagant, most loving step of coming to us, of making Himself susceptible to sorrow, familiar with temptation, and vulnerable to sin's disruptive power, in order to cancel its claim. God did not remain in Heaven and love us from a distance.

The fact is, God is with us, and the command given to Joshua is the command to us as well:

"Have I not commanded you? Be strong and courageous.
Do not be frightened; do not be dismayed, for the LORD
your God is with you wherever you go."

Joshua 1:9

The more we think about the fact that the God of the Universe became our "Immanuel", the more we experience an overwhelming sense of calm. No matter where we go, or what we face, He walks beside us, offering comfort, wisdom, and strength. This is nothing short of a miracle… and this miracle is the key to the magic and beauty of Christmas!

How have you experienced *Immanuel* — God being with you, in your life thus far? It is interesting to note that Matthew begins (**Matthew 1:20–23**) and ends his Gospel with the promise—God is with us.

> "¹⁹*Go therefore and make disciples of all nations, baptizing them in the name of the Father and of the Son and of the Holy Spirit,* ²⁰*teaching them to observe all that I have commanded you. And behold, I am with you always, to the end of the age."*

Matthew 28:19–20

All the **GIVING, GATHERING,** and **GAIETY** that man has connected with Christmas, pales in comparison to what God did that first Christmas, in coming to be with us as **IMMANUEL!**

Merry, mighty Christmas to you and your loved ones! May Christmas be a season of being spiritually close to God and others, whether social distancing or not. May you GIVE, GATHER, and have GAIETY, unlike any other Christmas, because GOD IS WITH US.

Socially Distant, Spiritually Close!

Sheryl and Susan

SCRIPTURES USED IN DEVOTIONALS

(Unless otherwise noted, the English Standard Version was used for all Scripture.)

Giving Introduction
- Isaiah 9:6
- John 3:16

December 1
- Psalm 84:11b
- Psalm 84

December 2
- 2 Peter 1:3
- 2 Peter 1:5–7
- 2 Peter 1:8
- 2 Peter 1:1–21

December 3
- Matthew 7:9–11
- James 1:17

December 4
- Romans 11:29
- Romans 6:23
- 2 Corinthians 1:20–22
- Ephesians 1:13–14
- Romans 8:39

December 5
- I Thessalonians 5:18
- Luke 17:11–19
- Psalm 103

December 6
- John 3: 16
- Romans 3:23
- Romans 6:23
- 1 John 5:13–15

Gathering Introduction
- 1 Thessalonians 5:16–18

December 7
- Luke 2:38
- Isaiah 26:8
- Luke 2:22–38

December 8
- John 15:13–15
- Psalm 25:14

December 9
- Matthew 28:16–20
- I Corinthians 3:9

December 10
- Exodus 20:7
- Matthew 1:21
- John 3:16
- Philippians 2:9–11
- Isaiah 9:6

December 11
- Psalm 96:1–3
- Colossians 3:16

- Ephesians 5:15–20

December 12
- Philippians 2:6–8
- John 1:1, 14

December 13
- Luke 2:8–12
- Luke 1:14

December 14
- John 8:12
- Isaiah 9:2
- Matthew 5:14–15

December 15
- Ephesians 5:8–10
- Philippians 4:8
- Proverbs 3:1–4

December 16
- Psalm 119:7–8
- Psalm 34:8 a
- Psalm 119:1–8

December 17
- Philippians 1:1–3
- 1 Thessalonians 5:11
- Romans 16:1–17

December 18
- Matthew 2:10

- 1 John 4:14
- Matthew 28:7–9

God with Us Introduction
- Psalm 145:18

December 19
- Matthew 1:23
- Matthew 28:20
- Matthew 1
- Matthew 28

December 20
- Matthew 2:1–2
- Matthew 1:23
- Matthew 28:18–20
- Isaiah 60: 3
- Matthew 2:1–12
- John 3:16

December 21
- Psalm 139:17–18
- Isaiah 49:15–16
- Romans 8:38–39
- Philippians 2:13

December 22
- Esther 4:11

- Esther 4:16
- Hebrews 4:16
- Philippians 4:6
- Esther 4

December 23
- Isaiah 9:6
- Romans 5:10
- Romans 5:8
- John 14:27
- Romans 5
- 2 Corinthians 5:18–20

December 24
- John 14:27
- Genesis 1
- Luke 2

A Final Word in One Word
- Isaiah 7:14
- Matthew 1:20–23
- Genesis 1:1
- John 1:1
- Joshua 1:9
- Matthew 1:20–23
- Matthew 28:19–20

ABOUT THE AUTHORS

Sheryl Vasso

*D*r. Sheryl A. Vasso is a full professor and chair in the Master of Science in Education program at Cairn University where she has been teaching and administrating since 1990. She is a graduate of St. Joseph's University (B.S.), The College of New Jersey (M.A.), and Immaculata University (Ed.D.).

Sheryl believes she has the dream job, teaching teachers, and she has done so on five continents! As a little kid, she spent every day of summer vacation "playing school", so small wonder that her vacation became her vocation!

In addition to teaching, Sheryl is Founder and President of Words of Worth, Inc., a non-profit incorporation that provides Biblical teaching for retreats and conference settings as well as professional development for educators, both nationally and abroad. Sheryl has co-authored several Bible studies and more about her ministry can be found at www.wordsofworth.com.

Born and raised in Bucks County, PA, Sheryl is Italian by family heritage, is in God's family, and enjoys chocolate. She believes, "In addition to God's Word, chocolate solves most any problem in life!"

Susan Weber

Susan Weber was raised in Central Pennsylvania. She went to Bloomsburg State College where she met her husband, Jim. Upon graduation, they settled in Bucks County and taught in the Neshaminy School District. Susan retired after 30 years in education where she taught all grades K-12, served as the Lead Teacher for Social Studies, and as the district's leader for professional development. She also earned a Master's degree in Educational Psychology from Temple University.

Since Susan's retirement, the couple has enjoyed traveling to Asia, Europe, South America, and within the United States. Her favorite vacation destination is to visit her grandchildren, and in the summer may be found on the sand in Bethany Beach, DE.

In addition to travel, Susan fills her days serving on several boards for local community non-profits, including Words of Worth, Inc., Hope for Youth, and the Neshaminy Education Foundation. She is also active in her church co-teaching a Bible Study on Wednesday morning. Susan and Jim have a great regard for missions and have traveled to four continents on missions' trips. She is also an active member of the Washington Crossing Chapter of the Daughters of the American Revolution.

Her greatest blessing is her family. Susan and Jim are the parents of two sons, and grandparents of six beautiful grandchildren. Susan's hope is to serve the Lord fully during her retirement years. She has been greatly blessed, and in turn hopes to bless others.

WORDS OF WORTH, INC.

ords of Worth, Inc. is a nondenominational, nonprofit Christian ministry that seeks to elevate the power of words, especially the Word of God. Providing biblical teaching, online and in person, through Bible studies, retreat settings, conferences, speaking events, and professional development seminars, nationally and internationally, Words of Worth, Inc. strives to encourage others with "words of worth".

Words matter…words abound. Every day we hear and speak thousands of words. Each one of them may have a lasting impact. With one simple word we can persuade, encourage, affirm, deter, wound, provoke, console, excite, invalidate, kindle, reassure, or inspire.

Words of Worth, Inc. exists because words matter, and God's Word matters most.

Visit us online at www.wordsofworth.com!

CPSIA information can be obtained
at www.ICGtesting.com
Printed in the USA
BVHW042009231021
619688BV00003B/7